’S BEAR GUN

RIVER RIVER BOOKS *Durham, North Carolina*

WILLIAMSON

Published in the United States of America

Library of Congress Cataloging-in-Publication Data

Williamson, Corrie 1986

Your Mother's Bear Gun / Corrie Williamson.

ISBN-13: 979-8-9881378-6-3

Subjects: LCSH: American Poetry, Environment, Family.

LCGFT: Poetry.

Library of Congress Control Number: 2024952500

Cover and interior design by Alban Fischer

RIVER RIVER BOOKS

10 Linganore Place

Durham, NC 27707

www.RiverRiverBooks.org

PRAISE FOR *Your Mother's Bear Gun*

"The world, I think, has planned for everything, save us," Corrie Williamson writes in a vibrant and devastating language that carries the beauty and terror, the joy and sorrow of living intimately with the natural world in the 21st century. Here are poems of "bloom and dissolution," stories that confess a deeper need for variations on the word *darkness* and the ever-present culture of guns as tools and threat. Early in the collection, she declares, "*To protect* // happens first and mostly in the heart, though precious / little separates it from possession." Such tensions inform this dazzling book as Williamson's unflinching imagination and keen erudition help the reader live fully in the contradictions.

—TODD DAVIS, author of *Ditch Memory: New & Selected Poems*

From the first harrowing poem, "Meditation," in Corrie Williamson's third collection, *Your Mother's Bear Gun*, she is on high alert—to the threats to existence that all beings face *and* to our capacity for courage and joy. In these poems, Williamson navigates the complexities and contradictions in our need for protection and defense, when the tiny leaves of pennyroyal, an herbal abortifacient, are as lethal as a gun, when a woman living alone in the wilderness feels both awe and terror at the cry of a mountain lion. Through gorgeous and vigilant language, Williams reacquaints us with the preciousness and precariousness of life on earth: a hummingbird's nest "in the apple tree's rain-chilled arms"; caddis flies, "each a tiny heartbeat hex"; ravens riding a storm like "black boats with slow black oars."

—MELISSA KWASNY, author of *Where Outside the Body Is the Soul Today*

Reading this remarkable collection I'm reminded how during hunting season of my high school days, any number of pickups in the student parking lot would contain racks supporting rifles, likely loaded, ready to perform their lethal and essential business as soon as the final bell sounded. I'm reminded of the trail I hike in the fall where the remnants of an apple orchard, gnarled and returning feral, seems to drag bear scat up from below the surface of the ground, like overnight mushrooms, and how that time a bulbous black bear—reclined against a trunk, munching away and eyeing me—seemed just shy of offering me a crunchy bite of my own as I paused before sauntering on, chest strained with joy and love. Which is to say, Corrie Williamson's gorgeous and familiar reflections are so tangled up with the landscapes of heart and wildness I'm reminded that they are really one and the same, and I emerge from the ice-sharp reverie of her work certain I won't experience so excellent a gathering of poems any time soon.

—CHRIS LA TRAY, author of *Becoming Little Shell: A Landless Indian's Journey Home*

YOUR MOTHE

POEMS CORR

Contents

YOUR MOTHER'S BEAR GUN

Meditation

Quiet, I say to the mind, and the mind says frogsong,
        bear emergence, death of all

salmon-kind, local proliferation of buried nuclear
        silos, tomorrow's breakfast,

blossom-riot of bees in pollen tresses, a child
        reaching into a sleek unlocked gunsafe.

May all beings be safe, I go on, and the mind
        hears only scrifflescutter of mice

in the insulation. May all beings be well,
        I insist, and the mind pries open

the eye to see one, like a fat suede knuckle,
        paw-tucked, slinking behind the stove,

along the corner and out of sight.
        May all beings know contentment

in hard times — the mind reminds me that mice
        are thigmotactic and hug a wall

like a mother's hip, ah, little cannonball
    of knowing. May all beings know

peace, I say, but the mind already
    is planning where to put the poison.

You're Hoarding Guns, I'm Growing Herbs

my sister tells my father after he bends
to pluck from her patch
of pennyroyal, age-old abortifacient from mint's

family, square-stemmed, toxic, crested
like a tropical bird with morning-purple
tuft, and he straightens, says, *You giving away abortions now?*

Later, she writes me, *I think he understood.*
And yet I cannot say what
unholy act, what cruel law or deed does not endeavor

to protect *some*thing. Not so very long ago,
my sister could have
hanged as a witch for her wilderness gardens

of nettle and hyssop, of yarrow and calendula,
her care for forbidden bodies and
snaring of bee swarms from pine branches.

Come spring, she'll find in the wet death-refreshed
loam spent shotgun shells planted
among saved seed of belladonna, mugwort, blue cohosh,

Queen Anne's lace, named, so the lore goes,
                    for the old queen's contest
to see who could knit a stitched flurry most like

the flower's fractal toothwhite face, though
                    she pricked her finger as she purled,
loosed a single drop dark into her own lace's clean new eye.

Three Bobcat Day

for Megan Blankenship

One bobcat, in the tea-dregs light of dawn outside Mountain Home,
Arkansas, and then — absurd, impossible, tucking its tailless bottom to scoot
under bush, another. *God,* you said then, *show me a third. Show me*
one more, and I'll believe. Here, in the spring Siskiyous, four does
dew-step the meadow each morning, timid yet timely, present
through the bloom and dissolution of cherry trees' flowering, through
the heart's slow settling of sediment, as the river prepares a bed
for the steelhead's return and a beacon for the strange brain that sings
to them of home when they reach it. Is noticing coincidence a form
of divinity, or worship? If not, a comforting mistake. *Oh yes*, I reply,
when you write, *Healed grows up around and inside you*, unruly as blackberry
bramble coming back thorned as ever. *Oh yes.* Though still, one dawn,
all the regular chorus and clatter, but only three deer in their split black
ballet shoes. And the mind, limber with lions, licks a moony claw,
bounds back along the ever so delicately darkened tracks through dew.

Whose Name Means Lion of One Color

I lower my maul to the stump to listen to call

        after echoing call from the tilted woods, and know
it is the Big One, cat of many titles: *painter,*

        puma, catamount, cougar, lion. Does a language

        have more expressions for what its speakers hold
dearest, or that which they most require to live?

We'd answer

        differently, me and the cat
screeching in the evergreen shade. I hope to abide

in places where she can, though knowing she walks

        my daily path I admit the trail seems
pressed by deeper darkness. *Darkness*: a word I'm always

wanting more variations for. Now the yowl

        and tremble, like the feline, keep coming back:
coming back to suburbs around Los Angeles,

coming back to the storm-sizzled Rockies,

to a neighborhood near you, coming back to families
bovidae and *cervidae*, coming back to me, splitting

maul limp against my knee, terms for *terror*,

names for *joy*, caught between my throat
and brain, snarling, becoming one and the same.

Hummingbird Tantra

"Everybody wants to let go, but how do you let go if you don't hold things?"

— DANIEL ODIER, *Tantric Quest*

Red draws their tiny eye, and every hummingbird
feeder you can buy blooms a plastic, stoic
ruby, effigy of flower, tadasana of red. Already
they have eaten me out of sugar, but forgetful today
I've left the sliding porch door wide, and on my couch
a cheery wool blanket, paintbrush red. I hear
the ruckus first, think, *bee*, think, *rattler*, come rushing
and find that small bright bird thrashing and
vrrrhing over the sofa, dashing itself on the western
pane, wings a frenzied blur. A dull, haptic terror
takes me: how can I catch it without harm to one
or both? That fierce little beak with which it
streaks after its fellow nectar-seekers? How will I not
rasp the lime-dark shine from its wings, like a moth,
with my hands made for grasping human things?
As I pull on my thick gardening gloves, somehow
it seems to still, lets me take it lightly between
thumb and index. What a pose: Woman Pinching
Hummingbird, no flex, no stretch, a great suspension,
a less than saintly clutching. Two billion heart-
beats a life, they say, for bird and man, and if that's

truly the plan, with this one's scared heart fluttering
a thousand a minute, what life is already guttering
in my grip. Without rushing, my mind above
the fear of slipping, I pass through the porch door,
my hand falling and then rising to implore the bird
to go, and so it does, rippling down to the apple
grove like a petal in a rapid, zipping me to the
moment as I stand gasping for air. Woman
Letting Go. The next day, I drive two slow hours
to town, buy a pound of sugar to feed this incandescent
timebomb, this short-lived, minute voracious god.

Oh Come and Let Me Tell Thee How Wholly I Am Thine

Is this the forest primeval? I ask the sugar pines,
walking among them, the ship-high firs

with waistcoats of fire-scar, the shimmering
alder, the laddered shadow of bracken fern.

But would the woods know themselves this way?
Do these trees shudder even now as neighboring acre after

acre burns and turns the barred earth between
their shadows ochre? The mind grasps so little

of itself, its Saint Elmo's fire, its Mariana, murmurations
and forgotten heartwood. Ash-light and autumn

make my sleep strange. The brain gets down
on all fours, scratching at all the doors it's invented

for itself. In bed, a blanket of smoke-scent, I dream
of Longfellow's wife, how, sealing envelopes

of her daughter's curls with the red kiss of wax
she lit her dress afire, and wind through the window

swirled her body into a pillar of flame on which Longfellow,
clutching her, singed his arms and face, and thereafter

            grew a beard, carried a staff of sorrow tall
and spined as a hemlock tree, which are all now dead

or dying. *How I am alive after what my eyes have seen,*
I know not, he wrote, though alive he was, alive in the red

            dew of morning, in the houseless wild, singing
still of that which goes before us into shade.

Bone Pilgrims

How terribly beautiful a name for the men who skulked the prairie
seeking the last of the bison bones scattered by ghosts

and coyotes to send to eastern fertilizer plants, the tall
fin-like dorsal process bones
that held up the great muscled mound
of head, the heads themselves ground to grow hydrangeas.

I'm on page 34 of Win Blevins' *Dictionary of the American West*,
which begins with *bois de vache*, or buffalo chips,

wood of the cow, used to kindle fire
in the wide arid west, before it was dry, too, of the buffalo.

It includes *bolo tie*: "one of the small
sartorial indulgences of the western male"
and *bologna bull* next to *bonanza*, a nice symmetry
there, and ends with "books won't freeze," a phrase
used to comfort cattlemen, reminder that the herd
is bought on the numbers in the ledger and not
the beeves frozen to tented hide on the prairie's bare plate.

I shut the book. Outside, the evening is saying things I miss.
The aspens flick their gold fingerprints

to the soil, done shivering with speech
till spring, though below ground they whisper
and rise, below ground they are one animal.

A few pages back, under "A," Blevins recounts the Ute's aspen tale
that I knew first from the man who hauled the poles

of his teepee behind his truck like long bones. It's the story
about the time the creator paid a special trip to earth
on a full moon, and all the living things trembled to show their awe,

trembled in homage, except the proud aspen,
who now, we know in recompense, quakes
whenever looked upon. This man tried also
to teach me a few Plains signs — like small bounding animal
looks out at you from safety. Like, we eat well tonight.
Like, moose. Or how the symbol for snake

looks a lot like the one for weaver, especially
from the distance at which one shouts with one's hands

at one's enemy, or friend, which is what one is trying to determine
while keeping, if possible, from trembling in the tall grass and making

large self-identifying gestures.

Missing

On the long drive, summer's dust
lies down, tired and tamped
as dough handled too hard. Soon,

mushrooms will roil up from earth
and bears dive into it. Tucked
beneath a rock, by the turn-off to the old

Alemeda Mine, a missing person poster:
Have you seen Fauna Frey?
along this gravel

Forest Service road no one drives but me,
and the occasional dump truck pulling
dregs from the crumbling gold pits.

Fauna. Our hair and eyes and height
the same. Home, the two soldered steel gates swing
shut, squeal like a pinned rabbit to seal me

inside. Fauna, whose very name means
animal, I try not to picture you in this river
through which I have spent all of summer's glint

seaming the bright needle of my body.
This wrathful thunder, this terrible bell,
always comes back to me: *girl lost* —

and sometimes worse: *girl found.*
Have you settled into the sifting
gravelbed of gone, slipped bloodless up arterial streams?

Are you, Fauna, weightier
than gold, and so precious
they'll tear the canyon down to sluice you free?

A Brief History of Preservation

I lie on the deck on my back, listening to the cragged,
woody bristle of a borer bee chewing the whole thing

out from under me, thinking of my friend Robert
visiting his childhood home in the mid-western

hardwood forests, how, as he tramped among the groves
and gullies, one old oak told him it was the same, and not,

yet he was moved to love the way the place had grown
up around his memory of it and was new. *To protect*

happens first and mostly in the heart, though precious
little separates it from possession. What effort

to keep from carving your initials there, like a spoiled lover.
What toil to prevent some other from doing the same.

Some tasks are small and easy graces — the way the lupine
cups the rain in its sleeves all day, the way my sister taught

my grandmother, before her mind went, two new ways
of expressing herself: *Fuck*, and *I love you*. Some tasks

you do with fear and tenderness together: axing
the cloud-bitten ice of the trough again and again because

the farm animals must drink, killing a crow to hang
on a fencepost for the sake of the fruit, or carrying

the bright-bodied wasps out of the house in the morning
hours when they are still too cold to sting.

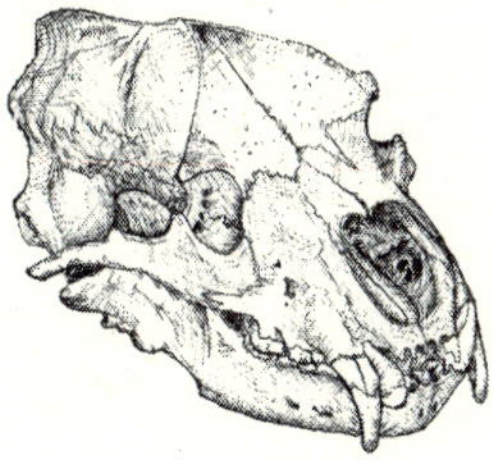

Using a generator indoors can kill you in minutes

I read on the big red and black Honda before
firing it up inside right next to the propane stove
because it is fall and the birds know it and wing
away just as the lizards in the woodpile know
and slow their scuttling while the walnut
knows and in the strange way of the world
seals off its own leaves to die by draining
from them the blood of the sun and the apple
trees know and unburden themselves and I am
turning their year's work into butter because
little in the world strikes me as holy wealth so much
as food jarred in clean glass which I am lucky
to find in a year where the whole unlucky nation
has turned to canning like the metaphor it is —
a year I spent mostly watching the wind
which churns now in the forest calving
limbs from trees to lay across the road
which will necessitate the use of another tool
that could at any moment lead me to dusty
death, that old unreliable chainsaw toothy
as a beartrap with its orange warning sticker
of an arm shorn of its hand though wouldn't
it be handy if the world itself came with
a warning telling us what is safe what

dangerous, crisp clear as one sweet apple
and one tart which is how you make the butter
best worth saving, sealed tight with a bright *pting*
that means tomorrow and perhaps tomorrow.

Kissing the Good Green Earth

for Jennifer Oakes

You lamented the absence of a human sound for longing,
like the loon has, like the wolf. I think of you reading
to your donkey the day he died, the passage where Odysseus
kisses the soil, how the beast moved away from you,
stood quietly in the clover, then returned,
wet your wrist with its bark-gray snout. The vet
was on his way.
                         Recounting this story, I saw
how you knew, beginning it, that it would leave you
weeping. You smiled, went on with the telling. You
didn't say it but I imagined you fed him something
sweet, then, a squat crystal cube, an apple, and leaned
in to catch the music of it, the thin sound like silk
of the inner lip against your palm, the rasp and
crunch of life's sugar dissolving, seeping, as you bent
your fingers backward, tight together, to avoid the teeth.

Season of Splendor, Season of Salvage

"The danger is not lest the soul should doubt there is any bread, but lest, by a lie, it should persuade itself that it is not hungry."

— SIMONE WEIL

October's days tack from cobalt to rain. The paper wasps
worship the short day's sun, hum at my windows,
drop in struggling pairs from the rafters, so busy before death.
At the meadow's edge, an owl lets me watch him
for ages, spins his head around 180° to remind me,

perhaps, that I am nothing. The deer wait until the first
frost, then eat the blood-bright, freeze-sweet rosehips.
The locals clean their guns, take their daughters
out to practice, praise her skill blooming like black
rot on the target's outline, and so she, too, is proud.

One morning high on the mountain, I meet the old man
whose son felled the big dead madrones on my place
and hauled away their rounds for his winter fire. We halt
our trucks in parallel on the narrow road, and he leans out the window,
camo fleece-clad, big drinker's nose, hands like mallets,

smiling into the air that swells with cold pine, and because
there is a place deep in my fickle heart for old men like this,
natural to me as breath, we chat, his rifle behind his head,
out looking, he says, for buck. *I seen doe and younguns ones*
but thaint what I'm after. He asks about bear sign,
his family's taste for their meat having made them scarce.

I've seen 'em here and there, I say, letting my inflection pool
with his. In a few short weeks we will loose our ballots
like children's wobbling boats on a bony stream — and what
will become of that? Whatever the month's end brings,
October, sepia tinter of time, holds it tight for now. We drive on.

My beloved teases me for thinking *malinger* meant a kind of evil waiting,
rather than to pretend illness, to avoid the day's hard ask,
the beckoning dollar. Whatever it may mean now, *aftermath*
once signified the season's second starry growth of grass,
a crop you might easily have not received, and might not even
have wanted, but must reap now, must not, bygod, waste.

To My Sister, on the Matter of Trees

Our father takes a chainsaw to the dropped oak
and it becomes a *cord*, beautiful word for the life
we burn. That old woodstove goes on warming the living

room from below. Look close, and there's still
no denying the ache of adding ring upon ring, years
of drought or plenty turned to heartwood and core.

This winter, my brain shuddered under snow,
believing for the first time, in the night, in my own
turning to smoke, lapis twist and curl above

the house: a breath, a scent, dissolution. Spring,
and I wait, ropy, unsure when to unspool
like the currents of sweetness the maples

weep on your land. You write to say, *I buried*
a squirrel drowned in the sap bucket. I write to say,
I cannot get right the poem about the man chopping wood,

how our days rise, cleave, fall away. You tell me then
that after five years on thirty acres covered
in black walnut forest with no harvest to speak of,

you cut the largest tree at the top of the hill.
The following autumn the rest rained down,
in abundance, their green-husked fists of seed.

The autumn my sister ate a pint of liver pâté, she claimed warmth like brushfire coals simmered winterlong in her veins

She cut the muscle and vitals
from the doe's smiling ribs. I smelled
its dark organ, buttermilk

soaked, combining with herbs
and the juniper berries — little
globes of stilled storm we plucked

from pine and leaf piles in the woods
behind the house — in the cast iron,
watched it swirl with brandy

and pack dense as gumbo clay
into her glass jar. She ate it
by the spoonful, licking the concave

face clean. This is the woman
who said her period was like
slaughtering a gazelle in the forest.

I think of it, the paste of another's
throbbing body, when my chest thrums
cold. Think of my sister's hands

gloved in harvest blood, her hair
dense and woody as browse, the sweat
off her skin rosemary, clove, and gin,

sharp as a bellyache and sour
as the wild overripe crab apples
that what she ate ate.

O Thing That Consoles, How Clumsily I Thank You

The wind curls like a wave
        into the elbows of the madrones,
looses great rafts of golden

leaves, bright as finches, chittering like rain.
        Apples abdicate their branches
with a sigh, plummet. On bright

moonlit nights I stand on the porch,
        listening. Say there is nothing
I can think that is not the moon.

Say that today, it's true, I lived without
        fear. And the day before that.
I put up pears, saw a skink with a tail

like soldered indigo. What could I
        have done to deserve this, and
is it possible that matters? The river

gathers unfathomable numbers
        of stones, keeps none, pulls
past its tall basalt boulders, down

towards where it all bends in the mist.

            The wind's the nearest thing
to divinity, with its hoist and howl.

If time and space indeed converge
            as intersecting planes, why not
god out there riding the solar

breezes, here nudging crows,
            making all things not made by man
listen, crumble, shudder, and bow.

*

Autumn and tongue-red pomegranates
arrive in stores, and I buy them
like I always do, ripe as childhood,

original fruit of the sin tree,
the knowing tree. The test now:
apples are to Eden as Jesus

is to a blonde white guy.
In my small paradise bears go
bellying along the apple trees' limbs,

which wink at the edge of my eye
in the bone-dusk-blue, heaven
stuffed with golden suns.

On the porch I watch a bear
big as a man, shaped, beneath
a gun-metal-black robe of dense

pungent hair, like a man, cruise
the deadfall, rattle the tall garden wire
and break in, hear his teeth crushing fruit.

The fire-capped tanagers
have flown. Yesterday I saw
my first pileated woodpecker, and it

barked like a squirrel. Once,
men believed that birds
of paradise existed only in the ether,

and had no feet. And that birds
wintered beneath frozen lakes,
snug as chambered bullets.

Is fall the season when disillusionment
begins — or lets go? The bears leave
their great piles of hardly digested

apple-shit all around. The rest heap
into wasp fiestas, into riperot
mounds: all those apples that will not

be trees, all those cooling stars,
those sweet firm tales we were sure
were true, and then consumed.

Reading Charles Wright's Sestets through a Lonely Week of Rain

Mr. Right, we used to call you, in the tart
                                        persimmon drama of youth.
You'd disapprove of my loneliness, my sad stove-stoking with dry madrone,
my waiting for sunlight like it would fry up
                                self-pity into something palatable with potatoes.

From my desk at the window, a hummingbird wears out its heart,
                                        pie cherries blossoming.
Get out into the wet, darling, you'd say. *Surrah, que sera;*
the mist is a shroud you may as well get used to wearing.

Your Letter Spoke of Rain

making currents rear, rock flour
silting the Nooksack with the cloud

of time's slow grind, the two men
jumping the Forest Service gate to be near

that sure unravel. Everyone knows rain
falling on fir and basalt is poetry.

They might remember it by the river,
where I find not that time or tiredness

are impossible, but rather that sorrow
goes from me like a foolish thing,

quits clinging like the stickseed burrs
my father called *beggar's lice* back east,

which are only trying to make more
of themselves. Funny, isn't it, how even

those born in the west say *back east*,
the blood's sunrise memory, accidental

immigrant's prayer. But who recalls
the rain when they shine their teeth

with its summoned stream, boil potatoes,
flush the trailer toilet at the fairgrounds,

thinking of horseflesh and prize
ribbons, of sharpshooter glory, joy or fear

of the father, of one they might touch
in the long bench seat of an F-150, skin

oiled bright by the moon — thinking, I mean,
only of all the other kinds of falling.

Fever Dream with Taricha granulosa

"Throughout western America, places with mildly toxic newts also had mildly resistant snakes. Meanwhile, hotspots with unusually lethal newts also had snakes that withstood staggering levels of tetrodotoxin. The two species were locked in a beautifully coordinated arms race of toxicity and resistance."

— ED YONG

I dream a cure. Summon it up from the cell,
little cameo of healing clad in a mucus sac. Wear it
like the cloak Pope Al III prized, made of skins
          of the fire salamander, which Da Vinci
said dined, in fact, on fire, and Pliny
claimed quelled flames by walking
among them with its stripe and slime.

          It is the newts with whom
I consort, the toxic rough-skinned variety
colored like silt who rise to sip
the pond's surface and drift back down,
          who mated, this spring, in writhing
bundles like a fist. A group of three hunters,
I read, set out the coffee pot full of water
the night before, didn't spot the slumbering
          amphibian there the next morning, drank
their joe *a la newt*, and fell down dead.

White-tailed damselflies drone the pond,
        translucent wings paddled with darkness
rowing their blue tined bodies over the surface,
where the female dips and dips her abdominal tip,
washing off her eggs, which sink to the bottom,
        become the beautifully named *naiads*,
scrounging in murk. Look, the world beats
down my door daily, syringe in hand,
insists the slow drip will never be enough.

        It's likely that Alexander's salamander
cape was, in fact, asbestos, the name itself meaning
unquenchable, stripped from the earth's throat
        in the mines of Tartary: fibrous, threadable,
silver and silicate as a sickbed's sheet.

For the Apple of My Eye, from Deep Solitude

The moon comes over the ridgeline
like a pumice stone, the day still warm,

Stellar's jays scolding as I pull fir saplings
from the meadow till my back aches,

keeping the wild from consuming
this gnarled orchard a little longer.

Which tree was it, I wonder, in her full suit
of moss, from which old Bill Graiff fell

and broke his hip, crawled to the house
to hang out a white sheet for the bush pilot

to see, though still he lay for days,
catching the pneumonia that killed him.

The saw in the shed, the deadfall high
in the branches, black widow in the woodpile:

all call out casualty for one alone as me.
The story goes that the doctor who lived here

in the not-yet-forgot days once treated
a man down at the river who had back-

cast a double-hooked bucktail fly straight
into his own eyeball by first experimenting

with an apple, burying a similar dual-
barbed hook in the flesh to see how best

extract it. The trees are in bloom, the moss
dripping morning's wetness in the warming

afternoon. If only you were here to catch me
a bright fish, smoke it over green alder

branches. Beneath the hum of hornets
we'd split that bounty in deepest secret,

like it might make us immortal — might
protect against the wind and the white

sheet, the softening of fruit, the body's own

ripe and scaffolded bone.

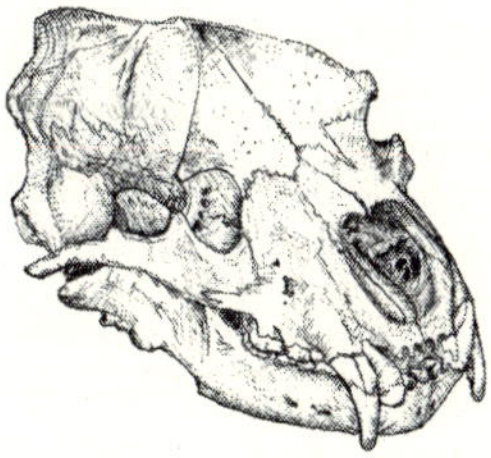

Keep Your Powder Dry, Little Sister

After a couple of pregnancies
that didn't give her live children
and two that did but nearly
took her from us, that was enough.
(Her second, I blocked her lungs
on the birthing table with a clot
that passed narrowly in time
to spare her, quick as first frost.
During her first, an emergency
appendectomy exposed that
bark-chewing tail of bowel
alongside my tiny sister, curled
nearby, pale cub.) And so there
were no more, though we, unknowing,
begged her for a brother. Instead,
we grew up with guns. If no big sib
would protect us, we had them,
at least, against rogue dogs that
bloodied goats, opossum and fox
that snatched chickens by the throat,
flame-capped woodpeckers wrecking
the siding, and all the fear we'd been
given. Like all brothers, they reared us
for war. They made our ears ring

with their shouts. They kicked back.
They said things like, I won't
let anyone fuck with you. And we
said yes, we need you, and cradled
them close, leaned our cheeks
against their cool and careless gleam.

[One moment it is summer, glasses]

One moment it is summer, glasses
of white wine in our hands as we hover
around Beverly's evening primrose bush
awaiting the promised 9:10 p.m. show.
Soon enough, I'll be barefoot
in the cold grass picking apples
and listening for elk hollering like ghosts
in their fierce and protective courting,
the season a lightless tunnel, the path
in darkness. But this moment there
they are: petals shivering loose from
furled cones, flicking out their buttery
wings into fragrant four-fingered palms.
Oh, I think, as we all say oh, oh,
there it is: the way to flare from shelter,
willing burst and die. We stand
quiet as the sphinx moths arrive.

A Brief History of a Hole in the Wall

Stephen Hawking's dead, I learn in the morning's
lean blue light from the Web,   which the physicist

        himself said connects us all now like neurons

in a giant brain. Children are walking from classrooms
today in protest. I'm thinking   of the time

        my father accidentally triggered a rifle while cleaning it:

the bullet he didn't believe was there passed
through the kitchen wall, out   into the living room,

        and buried itself in the exterior brick. Visiting,

I lifted a painting of white iris to find the hole hidden
beneath, a pale gray bloom   with a charred heart.

        A photo circulates on the internet of the students

of Livingston, Montana, holding hands in an oval
beneath the looming shorn   teeth of the snowy Absaroka

        range. You can see the wind in their hair and clothes.

My father learned to play chess when his friend Larry,
at thirteen, set off his shotgun   into his own throat

and face while climbing a fence. Always the fence:

its hook and noose, its stumble. Dad bought a cheap
chess set and would visit Larry,   who lived, teaching them

both together the way of the creeping pawn,

the heavy king, the sleek sideways knight. Hawking
said the brain itself was   like a computer: when the parts

stop working, that's it. There is no heaven for broken-down

computers. He also said the past like the future exists
only as a spectrum of possibilities — my father's voice at my ear,

passing on what he knew: *Sight, steady, squeeze between breaths.*

Old News

Chilled little fool, I smother the fire
this morning with too much
fuel, believing it ready for these cured

split logs, vents gaping, plenty
of good sucking oxygen
to make it snap. I feed it more

of less too late — the extra copy,
I hope, of the generator manual,
fragments of a torn-up fir floor.

That won't do; only brittle
newsprint and patience will rouse it.
Outside the hummingbirds whir,

wondering why I withhold their sugar water.
In flight, their tiny hearts may beat
a thousand times a minute, a heart,

by proportion to body, the largest
on earth, a heart liable to rupture,
to pummeled crumple. In the apple tree's

rain-chilled arms, their eggs nestle,
small as a bean. I'm thinking every day
is a prayer for kindling. I'm thinking

of children I won't have. My hands
in the stove's iron mouth,
my stomach moans and I lean in,

knees in the ash and splinters, spilling
out my breath to make this banked
day-cold blaze rise up and howl.

On Anxiety, On Chiroptera, On the Cabin Porch at Dusk

"The lowest form of animal life is the bat, associated in history with the underworld and regions of darkness and evil. Until now reasons for its creation have remained unexplained. As I vision it the millions of bats that have for ages inhabited our belfries, tunnels and caverns were placed there by God to await the hour to play their part in the scheme of free human existence."

— DR. LYTLE S. ADAMS, *in a 1942 letter to the White House*

My mind tonight's ripe with wings
as twilight: echo-worried,
path-blind, ricochet of timbred

hunger rustled from eaves.
Bats can live for up to thirty
years, gray about the muzzle,

pinions lashed and leathered.
What's in an old bat's mind?
Following Pearl Harbor, a dentist

from the desert wrote to Eleanor
Roosevelt of his scheme to strap
miniscule bombs to Mexican

Free-Tailed bats, release them
over Japan, where they would set
fires *likely to cause severe*

damage to property and morale.
In testing, their thumb-sized bodies
were frozen into ice cube trays

to force hibernation though
in the end, bigger bombs
released the bats from this task.

I wonder about memory's whiplash,
what trauma or joy passes
through generations or crouches

in the past-riddled brain. What will
stick, clawlike, like the tear in night's
armor, that space where teeth hover

near the clamor of the mind's
wooden city, its fissioning laboratory,
calling to itself. The belfry mind

that gongs and gongs, hinging
then falling around its own
tongue, its pendulum song of stone.

Goldenseal

Goldenseal plants are very small and live
in the understory of sundappled mature

hardwood forests, my sister writes,
where their veiny, palmate leaves hug tufted

white flowers and sprout a single thorny red
berry full of moist black seeds that may

take three years to germinate, to send down
those hairy turmeric-colored roots. She

sends me a brown glass bottle of yellow
tincture, for wounds, for aches in the belly,

for remembering how we hunt to rarity
the fierce and the frail, how we take apart

limb by limb the overstory to let the hard light
in. I have three minutes to drink my chamomile

clementine tea before I see my therapist,
who gives me this mantra: *That's only*

my disaster narrative speaking. That's only
my disaster narrative speaking. Goldenseal

yellows my skin. Sister to the buttercup,
whose bowl I plucked all those years ago

from the field to tuck under my chin. The name
comes from the yellow scar on the stem

that forms when the plant is broken, like
gilt wax dripped and stamped on a letter —

more to declare the sender than to keep
a secret, were we clever enough to have one.

A Spell for Traversing Quake Lake

near West Yellowstone, Montana, site of the 1959 7.5 magnitude earthquake

Valley of the drowned
I row my boat into, where

the skeletons of pines
skulk out from green

still water dammed
by what the mountain

calved atop the river.
I say the words which

science and not the
frightened heart offers

for explanation: *scarp*
and seiche, Richter,

epicenter, aftershock,
breach, fault. Little

spells of fact that might
dispel my sense there

on the water of the hands —
in icy, earnest grasping

carved from waterlogged
branches. I whisper,

Living goes on here:
the bighorns that brave

the slopes to browse in spring
along the road, cormorants

in the deadwood, brown
and cutthroat trout rising

from that submerged
forest to ripple the

surface with their jaws,
and snare the flies with

enchanted names like
drake, callibaetis, damsel,

mayfly, *caddis*, each a
tiny heartbeat hex, a charm

with limpid wings the jaws
drag with them below.

All in the End Is Harvest

Unable to produce the standard spring babies
that coincide with the lilac's fragrant unraveling,

my dad's little goat herd kids as always in winter.
He writes me with news of four sets of healthy

twins, but there was one nanny, he says, who
just came apart. Tried to put her back together

but unsuccessful. Gave the carcass to the river
bear. He doesn't have to say it — I see him, elbow

deep in prolapsed uterus, a sleek sunrise
cloud mass, the mess of it all refusing to hold

shape, to be sent back into containment —
the little spliced moon slivers of hooves

dangling. The bear, no doubt, came crackling
through last year's oak leaves and cold-crusted

soil to the offering, teeth clacking over bone,
maggots like stars in the night of his furred

throat, accepting this gesture of love's logic,
which says if you cannot save nor cultivate

a thing, then give it back — give it back
to the spin, the hunger, that good unending gyre.

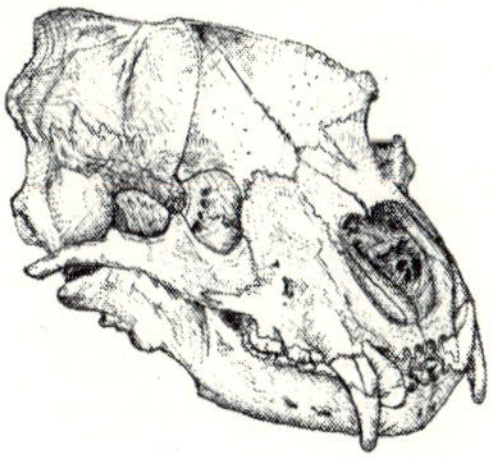

The Trouble with Water

The trouble with water is its storage
in sheds, the trouble with which
is etymological, *shed* stemming
most likely from *shade*, Middle
English's *shudde* which is reminiscent
of the body's rooted trembling
in fear or revulsion but actually
signifies a hut, the slightest form
of shelter, not to be confused with
the verb form, an older word:
sceadan, to cast off, separate, scatter,
more ancient still in its root *skei* —

to cut, split (where naturally we get
the split-spilling from our own blood,
or the place we stash split fuel for fire,
or the structure to which we are
secreted for punishment), or more
pertinently *shed* as land division
where like the language-makers
of ages past we go on chasing
one another down valley up valley

over hill and dale for bloodshed,
woodshed, watershed. The trouble
with water is splitting it among us.

Gun Ghazal

Oh, dad says, with a shrug, when we crack open the truck's
center console, *that's just your mother's bear gun.*

We tuck it away, in one of the house's many safes. My sister's
exasperated, though unsurprised, by her successful search for a hidden gun.

She's not worried it'll go off — but that one of us girls
will borrow the truck, not knowing it comes loaded with a loaded gun.

We might forget to check, after all, in the side door, floor mat,
glove compartment: we have no license to conceal a gun.

And what if some bored sheriff's deputy pulled us over, cocked
a trained eye past our shoulder — and there, ta da and gleam, the gun.

I don't hold beneath my sister's nose my pale, freckled wrist.
She knows. What would we say? *That's just our mother's bear gun.*

It makes Mom feel safe on a trillium-strewn hike by the river,
or a Sunday drive on dirt roads. That good, bright, ready gun.

We've always been told it can keep a family secure. And we're
just here for family, visiting home, had no idea about the gun.

Any cop in these parts would nod, pat the truck's roof,
and send us on our way, absently fondling his gun.

When I Consider the Heavens

"For they covered the face of the whole earth, so that the land was darkened; and they did eat every herb of the land, and all the fruit of the trees which the hail had left: and there remained not any green thing in the trees, or in the herbs of the field."

— Exodus, The Locust Plague

The pale wheat stalks on his black wool Stetson sprout
like a pheasant's feathers, farmer's plumage. He's telling
this story again and though I've heard it many times over
I lean in to listen: the autumn siege of Leningrad,
roads sheared like fencewire, Germans alighting
and sealing off the city, the crepitation of metaled
war not unlike the crackling of wings. Botanists
took flight to their vaults — the first of the 900 days,
where devotees of seed starved slow,
rose each day and among the tidy drawers
of onion, potato, tuber, rice, and grain, knelt
partly in prayer, partly in pain, counting, cataloguing.
We lean in. We sigh. He likes to say his Kamut seeds
came from an Egyptian tomb. None of us believe,
tempted as I am when I trace the firm, extravagant tresses
of the grain head. It is plain he finds sustenance
in offering us the scientists' dying like honey
from that crypt, into whose crystalized depths we peer,

wary, rapt, wondering if its still lake glows clover-sweet
and supple, or is stiff as stone, wondering could we dip our hands
to it, lick that old pestilence clean off our fingers?

All Forms of Landscape Are Autobiographical

A wing breaks the monotony of endless highway — a wing
        the length of an eighteen-wheeler, white
as a peeled boiled egg, a wing that will
harness wind and slice the flight from birds who meet it.

Who knows where the soul goes, after the light switch is turned off,
        Wright said. I had a lover who, not because he was a poet,
but because he'd seen too much shit in Iraq, called death
getting switched off. God at the switchboard, God bored

by the confluence of electric wires. *Red or blue?*
        He inquires, pretending not to know. Out here,
the snow drifts could be sand. The endless unseen flyways
of birds oxbow and warp like a stream in the cirrus whisps,

but could be the cracks in a dry arroyo's bed.
        My truck's shadow rolls along the wheat field's glow.
A gyrfalcon, resident till spring, cocks its silver face
as I pass. The sun goes down behind the grumble of trains,

its pastel fire flashing in the joints between coal cars.
        I don't know what happened to that man — only that he swore
his life was saved by snow in the Bridgers and the Missouri River's
green bounty of light and trout, his line switching the sky.

Circus School

"Thank you for visiting Overnight Caskets. This beautiful casket is available in various locations nationwide. Federal Law states that funeral homes MUST accept our caskets. Do not let them attempt to persuade you otherwise."

— *Wal-Mart's website*

for Emily Jungmin Yoon

Oh middle America, flat and fertile,
we've come here to sing to you a little,

these ballads of ours set in landscapes
a lifeway from here. After the reading,

the students praise the sesame chicken
and crab wontons at Hunan Palace.

One, with a beautiful equine face and long
ponytailed hair says he is twenty and engaged

to his boyfriend, but could never tell his family.
Another confirms you can buy an overnight

coffin from Wal-Mart. The newly widowed
professor sits quiet at the end of the table.

Another speaks with earnest adamancy
about Bigfoot, who slogs through the swamps

outside of town, often running through her yard,
frightening the dogs. He eats dogs, too,

she says, and has reddish hair, curly, built
like a wide receiver. After she pulled

her pug away from him in a standoff, she
went to town and bought a big gun.

Later, Emily and I ask each other — what stories
do we get to tell? Which ones are ours, which

off limits to us — though perhaps we'll don them
like dramatic eyeshadow we'll show no one

and blink at ourselves in the mirror.
In Saint Louis, with hours to kill

before our flights, we enter the City Museum,
visit the rooftop praying mantis. Emily takes

the ten-story slide in her houndstooth coat
and chunky heels. We sit among small children

and watch the young performer on the circus stage
toss pins, flip and leap through hula hoops.

I marvel that here is a craft still learned, still
held dear and desirable in the hearts of some.

For his grand finale, he stands on a medicine ball
taller than a cornstalk and whips out three

arms' length knives and Emily claps her hands
to her heart and he slings a stack of hoops round

his neck and before he begins he tosses a huge
red bucket by the door and says all these tips

help me pay off circus school and if you have fifty
to give you probably have a hundred. This

is my full-time job, he says. His neck begins
to shiver, the ball rolling wildly beneath

him as we lean in, drumroll with our feet
and the knives fly, all summersault and shine.

Adaptation

The concrete barrier
is what you hit, my friend
who's in construction corrects
me when I say *cement*.

Cement's what comes
out of the bag you'd mix up
for postholes, to build a fence.
You're going nowhere

until Highway Patrol checks
this out, the man at the tow
company had told me
on the phone. *That bridge*

is state property. The next
morning, I see the clawed,
blackish scrapes from my car's
bumper, hardly visible

even a day past when I
smacked *concrete* over
the icy Missouri, having
fishtailed side to side to side

before slamming the barrier.
The word is so evocative
now: shimmering tail that drives
forward even as it waves.

Put you into a fish the guides
here say when they mean
they will align your hook
with the desired mouth,

like my guide buddy Zach,
opening a beer for me
over the shellacked
outdoor bar at the Wolf Creek

Angler where the bodies
of pale morning duns are
preserved in the bartop's lacquer,
their small wings open.

The strippers, Zach says, came
to the cabin party in the deep
woods without an escort,
but seemed to know what

they were doing, exclaiming,
How cool are these guys?
before breaking out the coke,
wearing nothing but the belts

that holstered their tasers,
hair bright and metallic in the light
of the snapping pine fire,
pale and ashy as the wings

of the army cutworm moths which,
because the gleaming trout
with red throats are all but gone,
the grizzlies of the plateau

scoop from alpine shale beds and stuff
shuddering, meager, down their massive
throats because that's where the fat
is, that's how you veer to live.

Oysters

We are telling stories, Aran and I, slurping
oysters — muscle puddles in their moon cups.

I am trying out one about my father and opossums,
how he woke to a galled and frightened squawking

summoning him out of bed to where the hen
who refuses the comforts of the coop to roost her nights

in the blunt arms of the orchard's slim bare plum
and apple trees was surrounded by three creeping

didelphimorphia, their eyes lit wheels of refraction
in the December dark. He pumped the shotgun,

sailing the stalkers from the branches. This is only
a mediocre story, really, I say, as we prowl

the sidewalks of New Orleans, which are cracked
and upturned by the ancient roots of live oak

trees. The city sweats, red and white moths
blurring in the viridescent fronds, while river,

jungle, sea, have all the time in the world
to reclaim the plot. It's OK, Aran says, what are we

after all but polishers tumbling our raw tales,
shining our stories into fetish pearls we'll wear

around our smooth, craning necks, for hurricane
days, nights when the opossums come.

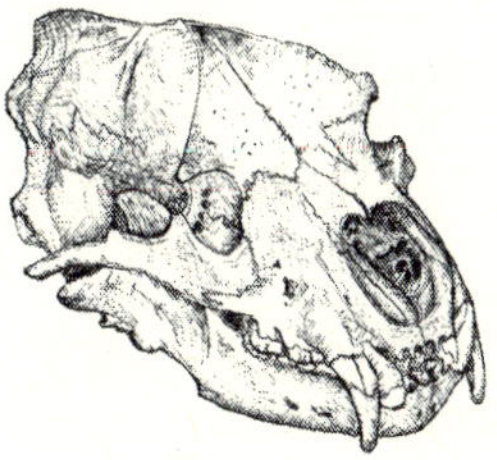

A Raven's Memories Are for the Future

The fat dumpster ravens croak,
shuffle in their scarabesque armor,
leave trident tracks in the fresh

snow linked by the whispy gully
where the long middle talon
drags. They show no fear, black eyes

tracking me, noting, I suppose,
the shape and contour of my face
beneath my wool hat, should I

prove harmful, somehow, should I
give them a reason to remember.
Never cross a corvid, they say,

and I've read how they recall our faces
for years, may pass their recognition
on to the chicks, tender seeds

of grievance clacking between coaly beaks.
In one study, researchers wore masks
of cavemen and Dick Cheney when

they captured the birds. Later, they
were scolded, followed, harangued:
recollected. Wise, I'd say, to hide their true

faces. One cocks his glossy head at me,
as if considering: How long to preen
this frost from the morning wing?

How much cold carrion? What glitter-joy
in the garbage? Who wrongs his kind,
and how best requite the grudge?

Thinking of the Last Great Herds Moving Like Storm Across the Land

Winter's a thin song and a somnambulation.
A roaring solstice wind blows magpies back
into the rough arms of aspen, and the aspen's
last leaves, October's gilt confetti turned
to gray paper coins, spear themselves
on the firm blue tines of spruce. The hoofed
ones become birds. Become stars in orbit
and moon-hauled tide, world of veer and hover,
world of V, of a little iron in the ear
to sing the earth's ragged veins. What can I
know of such anchor and such urging?
The elk turn as one body, raise the heavy soft
petals of their ears, and present, phalanx-like,
the white shields of their rumps, gaze
back over their shoulders. The world, I think,
has planned for every thing save us. It has
planned, after all, for these ones to carry
through winter's hard, bone-split days
the curled lives of the coming year, young
they drop when the sage smells like sweet
fire drinking spring's wet course, that they
drop as the tender shoots of new grass are

brightest in the mouth, that they drop as
the humped bears come up, rib-thin, ravenous,
trailing corvids like a high, cawing cloak.

Filling the Birdfeeder on the Coldest Day of the Year

with a line from William Stafford

Here's one small thing I can help keep alive:
chickadees flashing in the barred light
between the big fir's old branches,
which are bowed into shapelessness
by wind, snow, time. The bohemian
waxwings came for a day, found no berries,
flocked as one into vanishment. Ravens
ride the storms, black boats with slow
black oars. In the middle of the day
an ermine lithe as a snake leaps across
the yard, leaving the full print of its form
in the snow, divot and tail, divot and tail,
then dives, disappears, until the head
rises like a submarine's periscope.
Individual flakes gleam bright as mica
in the cold. I think of the mouse moving
low in the layers, how the ermine finds him
and tears him apart there in that invisible
subnivean universe, how bright his unseen
blood. What will I say when you ask me
if what I have done is my life? The fox's faint
tracks dent the fractal shards of sky.
The chickadees shiver themselves alive.

Hiding From the News

We watch winter depart from the lake's
ragged edge, wind blowing stratigraphy

into the surface from the west, raising
peaks and dips the eider ducks

and mergansers ride, then burrow into
with a frothed flurry. As ever, here's

spring in the rush of water in creeks,
the pussy willow shining along the bank,

who seizes her chance to be first to offer
the bee trembling the cold off its fur

an early spot of sweetness, their pelts
merging in the soft catkins. Tonight,

I'll dream of the lake as a bowl of igneous
glass my oar does not disturb though

I paddle and though I glide. A full moon
singes the shore, reveals the wet hide

of the moose that rears her head beside
my boat. If I am afraid, I don't know.

If I want to touch her, I cannot remember,
though I wake and long to tell you of her

swimming, endless legs poling beneath
the black surface, to escape me, maybe,

or merely seeking the long, pond-hair
grasses she dives to find, or another of her

waning kind. But you are sleeping sound
and the moon is not full, but sickle, slipping

through the blinds to hold its horn
of light to your reedy, upturned throat.

Mother Ghazal with Man and Bear

"The bear sees me as a human being."

— Woman in TikTok video

My sister wants to know: have I asked our mother
if she were to meet, in the dark wood, some warm other

would she prefer a bear, or man? Specifically — the worst
bear, or the worst man? My sister selects the bear. Or another

framing: cute bear vs cute man? *I guess bear; I'm married,*
she says. And, *How lucky I am not to be too bothered*

by the prospect of meeting either. I've gone into the forest
looking for both, she admits. In lore the world over, a mother

is made by love — or something stranger — between a mortal
woman and a bear. In such a story, something usually hovers

in the margins. I think of that Stafford poem, all the beasts
walking towards a gun loaded with darkness, how God, mother

of us all, lets it happen. But god of course is just a goat,
escaping in the high toothy rocks. God's a salmon, clover,

formed of honey and amanitas. God's a bear sliding down
the silvery branches who cannot reach the apple, his plunder

piles of twigs and leaves, a right mess. God has always
had a thing about fruit. But I digress. To sooth her

(my mother, I mean) we talk, as little as possible, of bear or man.
No darkness stalking here. No quarry. No fear, sweet mother.

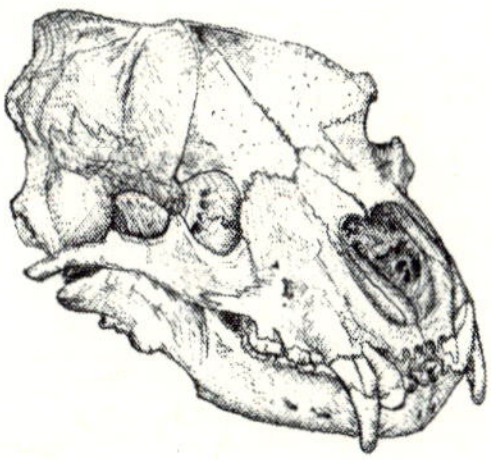

[Nothing blooms yet, though the willows begin to flush]

Nothing blooms yet, though the willows begin to flush
at the lake's still icy edge, to stretch their Titian wrist-
bones from the bank's wet crib. The scales of fir
cones hang wide, picked clean. This morning,
the silhouettes of swallows, my mouth full of bark
and sage, of quick-sheared darkness and gray noise.
My mother sends me articles about bears
with encephalitis losing their natural fright
of humans, eating apples on a patio mid-party,
walking into a classroom and sitting down
among the children. My boots breaking the thin
muddy ice-sheen, I imagine myself, now:
what a mad woman I'd have to be these days
to sit among the young of my own kind, plucking
shards of bone from my teeth and hide from my hair,
saying, *Take it, my winter-ragged paw*, saying
in white-hot earnest, *You have nothing to fear*.

For Having Consider'd God and Himself He Will Consider His Neighbor

George comes to the door with a petition to ask the neighbor
at the back of the loop to quit killing the foxes. *One of the reasons*
we all live out here, it reads, *is we love seeing wildlife.*
We appreciate their presence in our community. I'm startled.
This is George who plowed our driveway clear of snow
week after cold week. Who has been quietly building his damn house,
the cedar shakes, the knotty pine and stained glass, for a decade
after his wife left. I want to clutch his wide builder's hands,
send him home with milky waxcaps from my sister's bees,
with silly store-bought yams and branches from our lilac bushes
which are still too young in these long winters to scent the spring
with their nostalgic eve-drenched blooms. Oh, George,
will the tired scrag of the signature I make on the tattering page
change the mind of a man who put out those steel traps,
who gathered the swiftless form and sliced and jerked the dense
russet and gold pelt from the shrinking canine bones, who,
don't you get it, George, doesn't even own a single chicken.

Mercy Me

said the womenfolk where I was raised, and in my mind
mercy was a verb, the action reflexive. Though of course
the wolf in the kingdom of winter does not mercy
the elk. The owl does not mercy the hare
that has trembled loose from its delicate coat of stillness.
The word's been used since the twelfth century to mean
God's forgiveness of his creatures' offenses.
Such mercy is not what my father had in mind
when he asked me to take a pistol to live
in the wilderness. I didn't. That was not
how I imagined my days, strapping its cold weight
to my hip, a saunter to the river: *Good morning*
larkspur, good morning death camas and moon-
flower: I am more deadly than you. Would I
slip it into the crook of the quince tree while
I crouched to weed kale? And would I, after all,
shoot a bear eclipsing my doorway? Would I
shoot a man?   Back home, another gun
in the safe where my bedroom dresser used to stand.
Out there, the news, a loaded gun, returns again
and again to the loaded gun. Here
the old growth murmurs at night, the dark's bones
groan and creep. Once, barefoot in starlight

the color of gingerroot, trembling on the porch
at the unknowable's cacophony, the dog in a huff,
I wondered if the fear, in the end, would get me
first. On the long, hawk-spangled
drive east, all things appeared to me as bodies: the log
haulers piled with the fallen forms of fir
coming down from the mountains, chicken trucks
with their live cargoes crushed into hunchback
and the smashed daises of feathers from which
a dim red eye looks out. Across the frostbit
flatlands of Idaho, gleaming silver trucks piled
with fleshy potatoes: bodies, bodies, and on the radio
a story about a body unearthed from high
in the Andes, a woman's form arrayed with spear
and ax-head, a big-game hunter. I want to summon
a blessing on this vanishing year — but I forget how
this works, what to say,   in what order.
I'm thinking of my good Aunt who for all
those years and even after the chemo and the electro-
shock therapy tucked her pale delicate chin at table
and said with quavering but without irony: *We give*
thanks.   The moon's between the fir's ribs,
up there in the god-dark black. The fox still moves
in the roots and the rust.   You could say and not lie
that this is most of what I long for in the way
of distance and the way of desire: may the fetters
fall from all of us this year.   May the wild light

get way down in our bones. May we, without
requital, mercy one another with hands like wings,
with unarmed hands.

Uncle Kurt Talks to Bees

Because their nephew, at five years old, is undergoing chemo
for leukemia, because the world exists now behind glass through
which he peers, pinned in place like a soft saturniid moth, past
his own front door, my sister makes a film as her husband receives
their new hive. *Ohhh,* he coos to them, *Oh, you're so calm. I am here*
to give you space — so. much. of it, he chants, peels the slats free
in his lacy bonnet, and the bees' polyped sun-sopping thoraxes glow.

Maybe collapse will come for this hive, too. Perhaps they will lap
poison off a neighbor's crisp farm rows, drag this death-cargo
in their ankles and then at the doorstep of the hive dance directions
to that killing field, sending the rest. Or maybe a bear in his shuffling
might will smash the honeyed puzzle, bare the golden geometry
of nested horde, and drink the queen with her own mead. But now
Kurt calls these dewdrops of afternoon light his friends, and they
are wildly, deeply, newly alive. My sister giggles behind the lens.

Notes and Dedications

"Oh Come and Let Me Tell Thee . . ." the title comes from a letter written by Fanny Appleton to Henry Wadsworth Longfellow in 1843, shortly before they were married. Fanny died in 1861 from burns suffered when her dress caught fire.

"Missing." Fauna Frey disappeared in late June of 2020 in southwestern Oregon. Her Jeep was discovered on an old forest road, just over the mountain from where I was living. To date, no body has been found.

"Hummingbird Tantra." In 2020 at the height of the coronavirus quarantine, poet Lisa Russ Spaar began a bi-weekly poem writing project, emailing a prompt, and then the responses to it, to a listserv of over 100 alum of the University of Virginia's undergrad poetry program. Tucked away at the Dutch Henry Homestead in rural Oregon, I drove two hours to town, one way, to receive the prompts and send in my poems. The project was an act of great generosity and community, typical of Lisa. While several poems inspired by that project appear here, "Hummingbird Tantra" is the most notably tied to one of those prompts, and so it is, with many thanks, for Lisa. She told me after reading it that a hummingbird once visited the large red ear of her grandfather as he sat on a porch, mistaking it for a flower. He was, she said, honored.

"A Brief History of Preservation" is for Robert Petty, who will, no doubt, be mortified to have a poem dedicated to him that contains the murder of a corvid. This was an act I recall my father engaging in once or twice when I was very young, to preserve the garden and berry orchards, before he arrived at the point of letting the birds take what they wanted.

"To My Sister, on the Matter of Trees." The phenomenon described in this poem, the sudden abundance of walnuts, is known as mast fruiting. Unlike fruit-bearing plants, which typically produce a crop each year, wild nut trees may go years without significant production. When they do make a crop, in a mast year, all the trees in a given area — farm, county, sometimes whole states or bioregions — will do so all together. Botanists cannot fully explain how this joint plan is communicated by and among the trees.

"Your Letter Spoke of Rain," is for Jory Mickelson, poet and pen-pal extraordinaire, and inspired by their work.

"All in the End is Harvest." The title comes from Edith Sitwell's poem "Eurydice."

"All Forms of Landscape are Autobiographical" takes its title from the Charles Wright poem "All landscape is abstract, and tends to repeat itself." This poem is for Billy West.

"A Raven's Memories are for the Future." The groundbreaking and ongoing corvid study referred to took place at University of Washington in Seattle, with crows. The title comes from an article by Markus Boeckle and Nicola Clayton.

"O Thing That Consoles . . . ." The title comes from David James Duncan's *The Brothers K.*

"Having Considered his Neighbors." The title comes from Christopher Smart's poem "Jubilate Agno" and his meditation on his cat Jeoffrey. I thank my neighbor George for his snow-shoveling and his fox-protecting.

I am so grateful, and humbly thank, the River River Books team: Amorak Huey and Han VanderHart, for choosing and believing in this book, and making it better, and Alban Fischer, for his beautiful design work. Hugs and thanks also to my brother-in-law, Kurt, who not only talks to bees but draws most beautifully, for the stark and gorgeous bear skull that graces the book's section dividers.

Many of these poems were written during my time as the fellow at the Margery Davis Boyden Wilderness Writing Residency, from March to November of 2020, in southwest Oregon along the wild Rogue River. This manuscript is steeped in that astonishing place and would never have come to be without the residency. I owe a deep gratitude to that landscape, and to residency organizers Bradley Boyden, Frank Boyden, and John Daniel. And to the memory and legacy of Margery. Special thanks to Bradley for telling me the story of his doctor father and the fishhook described in "For the Apple of My Eye," and for teaching me that marvelous word, *thigmotactic*.

The majority of the rest of the poems were written in, and largely about, Montana and the high rugged country around Yellowstone. I am grateful to my partner Alex, and to his family, the Pyles, who welcomed us to spend the six months after my Rogue residency, through the first winter of Covid, living quietly in the small log cabin his grandparents built in the 1980's near the north shore of Lake Hebgen, outside of West Yellowstone.

And of course, my roots are in the hill-country of southern Virginia's ancient Appalachians, where my parents and sister still live. This book is deeply indebted to my family, whose lives are woven intimately through it. I am particularly grateful to my sister, for surely obvious reasons. This book is dedicated to her.

I thank all these landscapes and honor what I know and can know of their histories — their complexities and sorrows, their theft, their beauty and loss — and those who did, do, and will care for them and their remaining wildness.

Acknowledgments

Many thanks to the following journals, where these poems first appeared (sometimes in slightly different versions) and to their editors.

32 Poems: "Three Bobcat Day," "Thinking of the Last Great Herds . . ."
Boulevard: "A Spell for Traversing Quake Lake."
The Common: "Hummingbird Tantra," "Kissing the Good Green Earth."
Copper Nickel: "Meditation"
High Desert Journal: "Bone Pilgrims," "Filling the Birdfeeder on the Coldest Day of the Year," "A Raven's Memories Are for the Future," "Using a generator indoors can kill you in minutes."
Ecotone: "[One moment it is summer, glasses]"
Iron Horse Review: "When I Consider the Heavens."
The Kenyon Review: "Mercy Me," "Oh Come and Let Me Tell Thee How Wholly I Am Thine," "You're Hoarding Guns, I'm Growing Herbs."
Pleiades: "The Winter My Sister Ate a Pint of Liver Pate . . ."
Prairie Schooner: "Season of Splendor, Season of Salvage," "Keep your Powder Dry, Little Sister," "On Anxiety, On Chiroptera, On the Cabin Porch at Dusk."
The Southern Review: "To My Sister, on the Matter of Trees."

CORRIE WILLIAMSON was born on a small farm in southwestern Virginia. She is the author of two previous books of poetry: *The River Where You Forgot My Name*, which was a 2019 Montana Book Award Honor Book, and *Sweet Husk*, which won the 2014 Perugia Press Prize and was a finalist for the 2015 Library of Virginia Poetry Award.

She completed her undergraduate degree at the University of Virginia, with a BA in Poetry and Anthropology, and her MFA in Poetry from the University of Arkansas. She has taught writing at the University of Arkansas, Helena College, and Carroll College, and worked as an educator in Yellowstone National Park. She was the recipient of the 2020 PEN Northwest/Margery Davis Boyden Wilderness Writing Residency, spending seven and a half months writing and living off-grid in a remote section of the Rogue River in southwest Oregon. Her poems have appeared in journals such as *The Southern Review*, *Ecotone*, *The Kenyon Review*, *The Missouri Review*, *AGNI*, *Poetry Daily*, *Verse Daily*, and many others, as well as numerous anthologies. She lives in Montana.

RIVER RIVER BOOKS was founded by Amorak Huey and Han VanderHart in March 2022. Inspired by the idea that you cannot step in the same river twice, two poetry editors join together to publish (at least) two exceptional poetry titles a year.

CATALOG

An Eye in Each Square, Lauren Camp, 2023

Bullet Points: A Lyric, Jennifer A Sutherland, 2023

Dear Memphis, Rachel Edelman, 2024

A Geography That Does Not Hurt Us, Carla Sofia Ferreira, 2024

Pastoral, 1994, Joe Wilkins 2025

Your Mother's Bear Gun, Corrie Williamson, 2025

Field Notes, E.G. Cunningham, 2025

Encounters for the Living and the Dead, Jameela Fay Dallis, 2025

Antibody, Elane Kim, 2026

Fifty Mothers, Preeti Vangani, 2026

Scythe, Elizabeth Sylvia, 2026

The Visible Field, Zoë Ryder White, 2026